CW00481628

Gallery Books
Editor Peter Fallon

SWANS WE CANNOT SEE

Andrew Jamison

SWANS WE CANNOT SEE

Gallery Books

Swans We Cannot See
is first published
simultaneously in paperback
and in a clothbound edition
on 28 September 2023.

The Gallery Press
Loughcrew
Oldcastle
County Meath
Ireland

www.gallerypress.com

ISBN 978 1 91133 862 8 *paperback*
    978 1 91133 863 5 *clothbound*

A CIP catalogue record for this book
is available from the British Library.

Swans We Cannot See receives financial assistance
from the Arts Councils of Ireland.

Contents

for Rory and Gus

Come with me, Imagination, into this iron house . . .
— Patrick Kavanagh, *The Great Hunger*

So, take me in your arms again
Lead me in my dreams again . . .
— Ash, 'A Life Less Ordinary'

Listening to 'The Swan'

for Rory

Here is a swan for you, can you see it
with its wings all out and all noisy and taking off
on the still river backwater at Sutton Courtenay
where I've taken you in my work clothes
after I've picked you up from your long day
at nursery while I've worked to keep you
at nursery and it's ridiculous
how white they are and how quickly
you grow and how quickly they land
or settle or how the piano slows
to make them seem as if they're settling
and content and yet there are no swans
and you are asleep and the music has finished
and I've taken off my tie and you
are on my shoulders or want to be carried
or want to run ahead to point out to me
the swan because I hadn't seen it
because I was worrying about you being too near
the edge which was ridiculous and I'm
wearing my scuffed brogues and you're wearing
the coat and hat combo that makes you
look like a toddler-sized blueberry
and in the car on the way home you say
daddy play the swan but I can't because
I'm driving so you *doo-doo* the opening notes
which is ridiculous and you're snoring
down the corridor and mumbling in your sleep
and I'm talking about swans we have seen
and swans we cannot see, playing the music again.

The Muse to the Poet after the Poet Becomes a Father

And who, might I add, does he think he is,
plastering your kitchen in yoghurt
from a high chair, being waited on
hand and foot, cackling as you sweep the floor
beneath him, as you clean his face, his fingers,
with such care — I've seen those doe eyes before —
as here I stand outside the patio doors
in winter? What about this morning sky I've brought,
mottled and pink, the leaves of the copper beech
I've scattered painstakingly over the lawn,
the light of the moon I've jacked right up
so that it might seem morning at midnight?
Doesn't that at least remind you of walking home
by country roads at night in your teens?
I've even sorted out the pole star
for your car journey back from work alone
to that song you like about strawberries
in the summertime. What must I do,
what will it take to tear you away
from this new life of yours? When he wakes
you wake, he sleeps you sleep; the sickening smiles.
I can't abide to be abandoned like this;
you're just a glorified chauffeur, a means
of getting to the park, the swings, what he wants,
another of those sheep-shaped biscuits,
one more story. And how he calls for you
in the night. And how you go to him, stubbed toe,
not switching the lights on, how 'shush' is all you say.

To a Cygnet Swept Away by Floodwater

The Swan Upping is happening in Abingdon
but you're not there, little one, where the flotilla
of skiffs manoeuvres round your flock,
Uppers counting, measuring, weighing — no harm —
the few remaining, as townsfolk congregate,
witness from the bridge this spectacle
of sorts, but you're not there, and not the only one
this year of record absences, headline decline,
with more struck down by flu, attacked, or shot
by air rifle or catapult than ever. Perhaps
you're better off, baby bird, and you, nothing
but a ball of feathers . . . wee dote, what's possessed us?

The torrent that took you away runs through
my head all day: washing up, the shower,
bathing my sons, tucking them up in bed . . .
what made the water drive you from this world?
Aeroplanes' white feather contrails ruffle sky,
plumes fan from our diesel people carrier,
polyester garments flap on the clothes airer,
our kitchen gizmos hiss and spit at us,
and then there comes this vision of your nest
by the bank at Sutton Courtenay maybe
dislodging in a summer deluge
and there is nothing anyone can do
except there is something, or was, or should have been.

In Praise of Parmesan

The cheesemakers of Parmigiano Reggiano
employ a special silver hammer

to tap, precisely, each straw-coloured wheel
with a *rat-a-tat-tat,*

beat the bottom, the top, the sides,
testing in totality its tones, its tune,

to locate, listen out
for any imperfections,

decipher if it's ready,
to gauge its age,

adjudicate whether
this one passes muster . . .

What are they listening for,
their trained ear to the rind, I wonder:

the shuffling and huffing
of cows through fields near Modena,

a sweet relieving breeze
unsettling a tree outside Bologna,

first milk of the morning
striking a steel bucket at Mantua,

sunlight and rain
as they grow the grass round Parma?

Can they detect the farmer's breath, their sweat
peppering boots by Reggio Emilia —

pick up anxiety about the weather,
year ahead, livelihood, family —

or is it the sound that time makes,
the reverberation of passion,

the culmination of hope, belief,
of something cared for made by hand?

J M Synge in Crossgar, 2022

I am at the petrol station in Crossgar —
one of its three petrol stations, I should add —
where over-sized sports utility vehicles
predominate, mostly carrying one person
and that one person tends to be unshapely,
attired in loose fitting polyester —
which has the most convincing look of cotton —
yet such unshapeliness doesn't seem out of place,
and nor do tattoos on forearms, necks, legs,
ankles, of names, faces, all largely blurred
yet exhibited with what seems like pride.
In one instance a small child was dispatched
from such a wagon with a list, in a football strip,
running into the shop, before returning
with a bag of 'frozen chicken nuggets'
and a large bottle of black liquid
with seriffed red and white insignia.

Upon entering the shop entitled 'SPAR',
illuminated with innumerable electric lights,
I was greeted by a young lady, jaded,
old before her time, who wore a badge which read
'My name's Debbie . . . How can I help?' I asked her
if she could enlighten me about the history
of this ancient village and I regret to say
she wasn't as helpful as her badge suggested.
A little later, having walked the aisles,
I left overwhelmed by the choice of breads,
bemused by their lengthy lists of ingredients,
disappointed by the lack of books for sale,
instead I faced so many rows of magazines.
I was surprised by how distraught I felt.

On my way up the road to the monastery
I passed a band of youths, pale faced, wearing hoods

and chewing gum, who called out to me
some phrases I did not recognize, speaking
English, I think, in a most unusual manner,
a language laden with harsh consonants,
Fs and Ks and Ws and Gs mainly
and yet it wasn't in the Gaelic tongue.
The constant overcast weather, the drab
architecture, their flimsy footwear
seemed little to affect their vitality
as they passed me with much laughter.
The trees of the monastery tower
over the yellow-painted speed bumps,
and the path that leads to the clearing
revealing the mansion is pleasant, dappled
and leafy. A group of toddlers and their leaders
were having a picnic on the lawn, just cut,
sweet, almost sugary, in smell; it seemed peaceful there.
The monastery itself has been made over
and now comprises many magnolia meeting rooms
in which councillors talk of council matters,
hold 'away days' and discuss most things
other than religion. One of the most unusual sights
I beheld were the men and women, middling in age,
using the environs' woodland paths for leisure,
walking with exaggerated vigour
in luminous apparel which clung
to every lump of their flesh. Suddenly
my appetite left me, and I wondered
about their desperation. Stumbling out
through the monastery's woods I arrived
at the back of the War Memorial Hall
where I encountered yet more hooded youths
with smoking pipes who told me they could 'see
the fairies' and asked if I were one. They possessed
a faraway look in their eyes which troubled me.

I should have added that it was a school day.
A little later, after some repose
at my Airbnb that used to be a bank,
I walked out through The Square and down
to the High Street where the Post Office
had its windows boarded some years ago
and a row of shops had been remade
into a row of council houses. The takeaway shops
are busier than you would believe,
where frozen foods are dunked in boiling fat —
for longer than is necessary —
drained, then placed on polystyrene trays
and showered in salt from large white plastic shakers.
People queue out the doors of such establishments
even at midday, with the money earned
from work, if they have work, and there is nothing
to suggest they are anything but good people.
In one such place I struck up conversation
with a man whose face and arms were splattered
in paint: 'What are you ordering?'
'A cowboy supper.' 'And what does that entail?'
'It *entails* sausages, chips and beans.'
Then I drew back and didn't question him further.
As I walked along the Downpatrick Road,
the village's thoroughfare, if you will,
I was alarmed by the ubiquity
of the little hand-held black devices
the villagers clung to, holding to their ears,
looking at with furrowed brows, tapping, rapt
in their reflective rectangles, not looking up,
even while walking, or crossing the road.
The longer I stayed the less hopeful I felt.

One afternoon a hearse came down the main drag
with 'DARREN' spelt in an array of flowers

on the side of the coffin, seen through its windows.
The traffic had been stopped and the cortège
was long, with mourners wearing black. Folk
on the side of the street, mid-errand, had paused.
I asked a fellow if he knew the deceased
and he told me he did and that 'it was a shame';
'wasn't all there', 'sandwich short of a picnic',
'bit of bother with the Credit Union',
'fond of a drink and a flutter at the bookies',
'not the same after his Ma passed away'
were also terms he used before he moved on.

Soon after the traffic had started up again
and I made my way to the heart of this place,
The Square (a large car park) where stood a monument —
by which I mean a lump of rock with some writing on it —
dedicated to the inventor of the ejector seat.
I stopped a passerby to ask some more
about the famous figure engraved upon the rock
to which they replied, 'No idea, mate.'

That evening, my last in Crossgar,
I took a walk into the countryside
and aside from the articulated lorries
and speeding delivery vans forcing me
into ditches, at times, it was a memorable stroll,
whereby I took a detour into a field with a hill
from which I could see as far as the Mournes
and back down upon the village
and thought of Darren, and Debbie,
and the ejector seat, as vapour trails
cluttered the summer's darkening blue expanse.

A herd of cows rounded on me,
and the flashing lights of a combine harvester neared

as a shotgun shot rang out over the fields.
I could make out, inside a nearby bungalow,
a figure at a window at a desk, writing,
who watched me turn and walk back to my lodgings,
under the humming electric lines,
just as headlights of passing cars came on,
just as the rain came down, and I was coatless,
splashed by a fuel tanker as it hurtled by
and a satellite, not a star, tracked, untwinkling, the sky.

Teaching English

Hollywood would have us ripping introductions
clean from canonical anthologies, on tables
shouting *O Captain! My Captain!*, recitals
during penalty shoot-outs, midnight discussions
underground, smoking pipes and playing sax,
students riding pillion on our motorbikes,
breaking into song mid close analysis in bow ties,
leather jackets, half man half quotation-jukebox.

Waiting at the whiteboard of my white-walled room
I've watched the outside world's chiaroscuro
beyond railings all day. All day they come and go:
a blur of blazers, questions, answers, daydream
and clock-watching. I pass on what I know;
they pass through the corridor, into tomorrow.

'Harmoniously'

What was that word you learned this morning
at Radley Lakes as we peered over the railing
and saw the swan, ibis and cormorant
leaving each other alone as I told you
to leave the duck alone, swimming
by itself to the water's edge as I pointed out
the empty beer cans and why they're bad
and shouldn't be there, after you asked
about the noise from the machinery
in the neighbouring quarry, even though
it was so still otherwise, no other walkers
before the moorhen skittered across
the surface, before I told you not to scare
your little brother with all that shouting
especially when he's sleeping or trying to,
before we picked the unripe plums
because they looked so good, before
we closed the gate behind us with a click
and set off home for lunch through town,
through the busy town, with the people,
the people skittering over the surface
of their lives, like birds who share a lake
next to a quarry, next to a town of beer cans
and plums, shouting and sleeping. Go on,
what was that word you learned this morning?

To Abingdon

Quintessence of suburbia, roost
of aspiring middle to senior leaders,
hub of reasonably priced supermarkets,
apotheosis of the all-in-one
retail park, forum of first-time parents,
fount of first-time buyers, epicentre
of the steady, treasure trove of thirty-somethings
growing up reluctantly, still playing
games consoles in Converse and T-shirts
with slogans, consortium of the comfortable,
compromise's capital, mediocre's Mecca,
paradigm of the perfectly fine —

let us drink your ale, eat artisan produce
from your overpriced organic farm shops,
traverse your cobbled marketplace with prams,
talk, outside your coffee shops, of houses,
new play parks, government childcare schemes,
let us, without sarcasm, praise your Christmas lights,
appreciate your one-way system,
the multi-storey car park with one hour free.
Grant us nothing spectacular, console us,
in our cries for attention, with anonymity.

Youth Club

On a trip to Dundonald Ice Bowl once
run by the Presbyterian Church
I'll never forget I found my brother
with his mate Mervyn and another
huddled beside the rink — I kept my distance —
unveiling a white and blue pack of Regal Filter
and a plastic see-through lighter,
conspiring. I never knew he was a smoker.

I slunk away, but still see the film of the box,
its silver foil, the neatly stacked sticks,
hear the dance music blast, skates' blades
scratching ice, the pins' cavalcades
of tumbling, strobes from arcades and disco.
What else? What else was there I'd yet to know?

Mortgage

I came across it cleaning out the shed,
then realized it was the shed,
so, too, the skylights, bifolds, copper beech,
doves on the lawn, rats darting through the mulch.
My son wears an invisible coat stitched
with its terms and conditions; he sleeps in it.
Each meal I cook is laced
with its cloying contrast of hope and doubt.
When I stand at the end of the garden
and the stars are out, mind clear, alone,
there's only so long
before it rears between each constellation.
Sometimes I've seen it on a supermoon,
a sickle moon, my breath in air, condensation
in the ensuite, the limescale's pattern,
it gushes from the tap in hard water,
accumulates in pipes, clogs the gutter.
Here it is: crumbling grouting on the patio
between the slabs of Indian sandstone,
settling cracks in the extension's ceiling:
insidious, precious; static, creeping.
Survey this front to find it buckling its way
through my body — day after mortgaged day —
seeping from my eyes, all over my face.
If you listen you can hear it in my voice.

In Praise of Artisans

It would be something, to build a staircase
by hand: pick wood, measure out risers, space
between spindles, treads, the angle
of the banister, and dead level
position of the balustrades, the newel post precise,
spot on and sturdy, its cap cut to size,
conforming to proportions just
so, warpless, sanded splinterless, sans snags, just

so nobody could fault it, state it wouldn't pass
for a staircase. They could stamp boots
all over it, up and down, examine, in cahoots,
its joints and lines with a magnifying glass
for kinks and twists and crooks. Taking it apart
would only serve to reinforce its art.

Lines from a Dream

In my dream last night you were there with me
in a first-floor flat on the Royal York Crescent
and somebody said, 'Love is never finished.'

Last night I dreamt about us in a flat:
one of those white late-Georgian ones in Bristol
and somebody said something about love.

We were on the Royal York Crescent,
high up in a flat, it was morning:
'Love never finishes' I could have sworn somebody said.

'Love never finishes' has been going around
my head all day — a line from a dream
from last night — you were there with me in Clifton.

Was it 'Love is never finished' or 'Love
never finishes' that someone said in that flat,
last night, by the big windows in my dream?

Last night I had a dream about a line about love
and when I woke this morning I said,
'In my dream last night I wrote you a poem.'

So original at the time, that line
in my dream, last night, about love never finishing —
like the struggle to articulate a dream about love.

I've wanted to go to sleep tonight and find you there —
Clifton, that fancy flat with the big windows
above the trees — and tell you the rest

late in the white Georgian morning.

The Poet's Wife

The poet's wife is knitting in the other room;
what she's doing she isn't doing for herself.
For yet another evening she is by herself.
Gone midnight, she doesn't start or wake
when the poet stubs his toe clambering
into bed, the bathroom light left burning.
She's slow to anger, the poet's wife, works full-time,
is not slapdash. She is well read, and classically trained

but, humble, doesn't like to talk about it.
Her swooping handwriting is inscribed
in all the cards she never forgets. She never forgets
to stop: eating, drinking, talking. She irons
the shirts that are not hers. She always wins
at Scrabble. She has a way with words.

The God of October Half-term

I bring you fish and chips on the first Friday night,
chasing your child around the kitchen
until you're not sure whether what you see
is slowing down or speeding up, certain
this is more like life. I bring you your happiness,
family. I bring you a stitch, exercise
in the morning before breakfast. Breakfast,

I bring this undisturbed, at your own pace,
with sliced ripe bananas in it, quietly.
I bring the baking of your own bread,
an upside-down cake with the going-off fruit,
black treacle, golden syrup, brown sugar, butter.
Sausages will be brought as you please,
the fancy ones from the farm shop, defrosted,
roasted, with vegetables and gravy on a Sunday.

I bring your wife coffee, coffee with your wife,
a sonogram of your second child. A day out
at a palace named Blenheim will be proffered,
a miniature railway, ham sandwiches
at a picnic table. Tubs of ice cream
will be brought to you, outside, wearing coats.
A circus performer, and man twirling fire
in the great courtyard will be provided, gratis.
I bring you rain just as you've left for home.

I bring you two tons of garden mulch,
a shovel and a trowel for a toddler,
the clear-headed bliss of manual labour.
Successful potty training I bring you,
pungently and shiningly and well formed
from your firstborn, smilingly, with stickers.
I bring you time past and time present
and a review of two new books on Eliot

in Sunday's supplement you'll have time to read.
I'll bring an extra hour, a bit more light,
and wind the clock backwards before I leave.

Heaven as a Newsagents

In heaven there is Mary Miscampbell
selling Turkish Delight and Gold and Silver
Benson and Hedges, looking down, over
glasses, mispronouncing Raspberry Ruffle
and becoming irate at too many wains
for being there, amid Mars Bars, Sherbet Fountains,
Brannigans Roast Beef and Mustard crisps, thick cuts.
There is dark wood, a hum of cigarettes,

a whiff of wheaten bread from her kitchen out the rear.
It's cramped, badly lit, the front is frosted over
with an advert for Lambert & Butler. Cash register
and shop-door bell ring. My grandparents will be there
clutching *Down Recorder* and *Mourne Observer*,
gossiping about who's died, the endless weather.

Break

I'm watching myself through the big windows
of the primary school, on the mat with the others
in the corner in our red jumpers
and white collars and grey trousers and eyes
and mouths open, tilted upwards, being read to
by Mrs Kelly, enthusiastically,
by the bookshelves under the alphabet banner,
in a colourful pullover and dangly earrings
driving daily from Belfast in a blue Ford Escort.

And I watch him (myself that is), chubby, gingery,
seven, flit his gaze to the window,
freckles and bed-hair and buck-teeth, to watch
the tops of trees in the monastery
swaying and then not swaying
across the road, the sunless sky, the little terrace
of single-storey houses, an old man going
slowly to claim his pension from the Post Office,
probably, or to the bookies, or the bakery
for cream buns, or for a check-up maybe,
or soup vegetables from Colgan's or a pound
of stewing steak from Withers', perhaps,
or a paper from Miscampbell's in The Square,
or taking a book back to the library on the bus,
or a packet of fags, golden or silver,
or to say his prayers in chapel or church,
the Catholic one or the Protestant one,
the one where you cross yourself or the one
where you don't, the one which gives mass
and the one with sermons, the one with confession
and the one without, the one which hails Mary
and the one which most certainly does not,
the priest or Rev, sacred heart or burning bush,
the good one and the bad one, the one you are,
and the one you are not and that's just that —

Andrew, stay with us as storytime ends, break time
begins, and the headmaster delivers the crate
and they sit well behaved, with heads bowed,
drinking their milk from glass bottles through straws
like the children in the blue and yellow uniforms
on the other side of town, with Irish-sounding names.

Badminton Water Fight in the Garden, January

And who says you can't play badminton
in the garden with your son in January
if he wants although he's only three
and can't hit the shuttlecock and doesn't know the rules
or enough numbers to keep score,
would rather stamp on the net, stamp on it
and beat the racket into the soft ground
shouting 'TENNIS!' before dragging it along
the patio slabs despite your protestations,
calling for the water pistols, the blue one,
and the red one, and to fill it, and to fill it
until it bubbles up over the top, gushes
ice-cold over your hand and trousers and shoe?
There was a time this would have bothered you.

Watching 'Africa' after Dinner with my Two-year-old

Male giraffes fight by swinging their necks
at each other in a bid to claim territory,
the defeated facing exile. There is blood
and slow motion close-ups of each bout. One
collapses, its neck whiplashed against
the hard hotness of the savannah floor.
There is a cloud of dust. Big crickets
climb into the nests of birds in a bid
to try and eat their young; without success
they fall and are eaten, often, by their own.
The golden catfish is the most solitary
fish on the planet, living underground
in a lake the size of three jumbo jets,
if you place them end-to-end. Blind,
they know the world only by touch;
their lives are lived without daylight.
There is a constant struggle to eat, drink,
find shelter, not get eaten or driven away, to protect.
An ostrich leads its chicks through heat —
unthinkable in a quest for a waterhole.
Meerkats are protected for most of the year
by drongos; but, at times, this bird
will trick them and steal their prey.
Kalahari translates as *land of great thirst*,
we're told, against high definition panoramas.
Leopards kill steenbok and stash them in trees.
I ask him *'Are you tired? Have you seen enough?'*
He doesn't argue when I turn it off.

Breakfast Tomorrow Morning

While he sleeps cluster bombs have fallen
and there is smoke and noise and fire and people
in a rush to the station where there is no room
on the trains and men are insisting on women
and children first. High streets, grand high streets,
busy high streets, that took many men many years
to construct have emptied and tower blocks are smoking,
struck by indiscriminate missiles,
and the air whizzes and old stone is newly pocked,
all sorts of shouting, and car alarms go off
while war photographers take shots
for tomorrow: one of a father beside his son
on a stretcher beneath a bloodied sheet,
and it's not clear if the son is sleeping
or not waking up and tomorrow

when we have breakfast and he wants the book
with birds in it again and again I will read it to him
and I won't be angry or glance at the clock
as I say, and then he says — reciting his favourites —
sparrowhawk, waxwing, hoopoe, peacock —
silly peacock, silly, silly peacock —
American goldfinch, lappet-faced vulture,
bird-of-paradise . . . I'll drive him
to nursery, under a sky that's overcast
and here, at least for now, uneventful
and nothing he'll ask will be too much trouble.

Cygnus

for Aimee

Can you make out this skeleton constellation, can

you see it spread its stars as if in flight, yet

go nowhere, suspended in the up-there airless white/black

nothing of night, in intersecting lines? So

unusually striking — so slight, simple. Cygnus,

swan, single, constant, burning totem bird of our togetherness.

A Short History of the Potato

Boiled, it steams into the world on a plate
on a Sunday at the head of the table
with butter after church before a man
a father of five in a shirt and tie
and polished brogues and Old Spice with rough hands
from dairy farming stock near the north coast
with a glass of red and carrots and beef
who has a separate dish for the peelings
and a son who prefers them roasted
and partial to storming off when baited
by siblings about his weight or love objects
encountered at the Presbyterian youth club
the night previously and then there is mash
in a Pyrex dish adorned with a sprig of parsley
nobody eats or eats out of bravado
or boredom like the blond-haired brother
who is also partial to boiled above roasted
like the father who was reared on nothing else
in a family of eleven who would have marked
the start of summer by the first bag —
spoken of almost reverentially —
of Comber Earlies — their skin, the flavour —
or so it is reported, unlike his children
who eat them processed in waffle shape
with fish fingers made by the same
international frozen foods giant
with factories in Australia,
Europe and America, at the time of writing,
a time in which you'll find the potato
in many guises: farled, hasselbacked, boxtied,
puréed, crisped, chipped, hashed, smashed,
French fried, triple cooked, cooked in beef fat,
champed, colcannoned, even volutéd, foamed,
not to mention the rosti which the aforementioned
father had with a ribeye and red wine sauce —

'pretentious, too pricey and far too rich' —
at his sixtieth birthday at a restaurant
which is no longer there on Shaftesbury Avenue
which is in Ulster renowned for its fry
which is known for its potato bread (fadge)
which the wife of the father would send
to the roast potato son when he moved away
to London where people who weren't from Ulster
would say 'potato, potato, potato' in an Irish
You'll-never-get-me-Lucky-Charms kind of accent
because they thought it was amusing
perhaps, in the kebab shop at the end of the night
where the chips were not satisfactory
unlike the kind he'd have in the back of the Montego
with his sister in the car park at Carryduff Shopping Centre
from the chippy whose name has been lost
but by all accounts was an amusing play
on words such as Fryer, Golden, Chip, Village, The
covered in salt and vinegar waiting on their mother
in school uniforms and unargumentative

Unargumentative, unargumentative
unlike the child (two at the time of writing)
that boy in the back seat who became a man —
after consuming an unrecorded number
of potatoes in their various forms —
went on to have with a woman, who
also enjoyed her potatoes, roasted
with a little seasoning and sprig of thyme
or rosemary or both and maybe even
an ever-so-slightly squashed garlic clove
on a Sunday with some meat and gravy
and maybe even some red wine and maybe even
their son who (two at the time of writing)
might not feel like not eating, who can, to be fair,

be relied upon to eat potatoes —
pending statistical analysis —
more than any other food type
and when asked to choose between chips or mash
says *chips and mash* which leads us to believe
he is his father's father's grandson

He is his father's father's grandson
the same grandfather who is remembered
for buying his son in punts a small overpriced
polystyrene tray of chips in Dublin
at one of the vans beyond the turnstiles
on the old Lansdowne Road covered
in vinegary ketchup and so much salt
it gave the sauce a grainy texture but how
good they were in the top tier of the West Stand
the day that Ulster won the European Cup
in 1999 despite the distance from the pitch,
the son's dislike of heights, the lack of conversation,
the throng on the way out to the Dart, the stench
of Guinness and cigarettes everywhere,
accents thick as cold butter on bread, and faster
and faster such memories come back to him
and you can picture them, the two of them,
arriving too early, taking their cheap seats
in the top tier of the empty stadium,
looking out on a city that is not theirs,
far from home, and yet not that far, really,
on a Saturday, in their coats, huddled, not losing
their return tickets, eating chips and waiting
for everything to start and everyone to be there,
early because they were afraid of being late,
the son oblivious to the memory happening to him,
filling his face, and not saying thank you

Thank you thank you thank you thank you thank you
is what the father demands the child (two
at the time of writing) says when given a crisp
or other potato-based snack such as
a Pom-Bear or Quaver, for example,
or even a standard Walkers Ready Salted
which the father would eat in ungodly
amounts as a teenager, and which he bought
from a vending machine in the John Radcliffe
during the son's delivery
which he ate while wandering under the trees,
painlessly, which cannot be said of the mother,
who was whisked into theatre
for an emergency caesarean,
and was given two slices of toast with butter
and a cup of tea at half-three in the morning
as the child fed and did not feed and fed
and did not until it was fine, and everything
else was fine until it was not, again, and so on

And so, on to the past, let us turn
to a hillside of the Andes in Peru, say
5000 BC, give or take a few
thousand years, the morning sun
caught in the dew of the mountain grass,
the day yet to heat up, the air cool,
and a child is digging for fun, maybe,
around some flowers that are pink
and some white and some purple before
he pulls out a lump, caked in soil, and another
and another and doesn't know what they are
because they could be stones or some kind of egg
and he smashes one against a rock and he chops
another in half and he sniffs it, and prods it
tentatively, and it is months before

he goes there again, and there are more
flowers, and he tries to bite one but hurts
his tooth and anyway it tastes of soil,
so he takes it to his father as if to say
what the hell is this anyway and the father
takes off his feathery headdress, and long red robe
and armour and looks a bit closer, and grunts
and throws it into a boiling pot — unpeeled,
unsalted, whole — to see what will happen

And what happened is recipes: *papa
a la Huancaína, causa rellena,
lomo saltado, chuño, salchipapas,*
and a Spanish invasion in the sixteenth
century, the conquistadors stashing
their ship full of spuds to bring relief
from scurvy, bringing them back
to Europe, and then a ban
in France for fear of the spread of leprosy
and then what happened
was Antoine-Augustin Parmentier

Let us turn to Antoine-Augustin Parmentier,
let us turn to the eighteenth century,
let us turn to his prison cell
in the Seven Years' War, the bare walls,
the hard, cold floor, a tiny window,
a rattle of keys, the clank of the door,
and a plate of boiled potatoes thrust through,
day after day until he realized
he wasn't dying, let us turn to his release,
let us turn to his campaign to grow the tuber
instead of grain, let us turn to the farmer
who eventually gave in, let us turn to their
first harvest, let us turn to their children

sleeping soundly after dinner, let us turn
to the bouquet of potato blossoms
around the hat of Marie-Antoinette,
let us turn to the armed guards surrounding
his potato patch at Sablons
to make them seem worth stealing,
let us turn to the Faculty of Medicine
in Paris 1772
and their praiseworthy declaration,
let us turn towards the ghosts of famines
that never were, so when we turn
to fries in the car at the drive-thru,
or a bag of crisps with a pint at the pub,
or *patatas bravas* at the pop-up tapas today,
we might (in fact, let us) turn to him,
Antoine-Augustin Parmentier

And we only can surmise that Antoine-Augustin
Parmentier would have approved
of 'The Potato Eaters' by Van Gogh,
his only ever portrait of a group, Nuenen,
at the end of the nineteenth century, unlike
the critics of the time who implied
the colours were too dark, the faces riddled
with mistakes, but — and we can only surmise —
Parmentier would have enjoyed the hands
of the figures, in particular, how gnarled
they seem, fresh from digging the patch,
the oil lamp, the clock striking seven,
the steaming pile of potatoes, the pouring
of the coffee, the table linen,
the peasant family living on their produce,
their humility, their grace, their ordinariness,
but, of course, we can only surmise all this

In the way we can only surmise
how similar this Van Gogh scene
was to a cottier's cabin, say,
in Cork, let's say Youghal, the town
where William H McNeill argues (1949)
Walter Raleigh was not the first importer
of the spud to Ireland, but instead proposes
that it probably was the Spanish passing through,
citing lack of evidence for the explorer's case,
hinting he was propaganda for the British cause,
the English war hero helping Ireland —
and other sources don't rule out how some got washed
ashore from the wreck of the Armada either —
but anyway, back to this Corkish, Van Goghish
Irish cottier's cabin, the night before the rot sets in,
the joviality around the dinner table,
the talk of the town, how the wheat and barley,
the oat and the flax
are shaping up this year, the peat fire embering
in the hearth,
before the first cottier wakes, washes, walks out
to go about his day, inspect his crops
wondering about the little lesions on the leaves,
the whitish growth, the cold weather,
thinks how good is the good old Irish Lumper

How good is the good old Irish Lumper
and who could blame him, after an eight-fold
rise in population across two centuries,
a republic of bellies full of carbohydrate
cooked, according to William Wilde —
father of Oscar and chronicler
of that nation's gastronomic backwardness —
'with or without the bone or the moon'
which meant half-cooked

for slow release as they worked the fields
for the potatoes they'd harvest, they'd eat potatoes
in order to harvest potatoes in order
to eat potatoes and so on
and largely just the good old Irish Lumper
and such unseasonably wet weather

And such unseasonably wet weather again
he thinks to himself, as he detects a nasty
odour from the plant, the next day,
and the next day, and the next day,
as the rain keeps coming or doesn't go
and the sun won't dry the fields, won't check
this fungus, this *phytophthora infestans*
the botanists would call it

Just as the botanists would call
the potato *solanum tuberosum*
but what help were the botanists
and Latin terms to the cottier
and his community of cottiers
and this country of cottiers
as the panic set in at the speed of blight,
the speed of spores and whitish growth,
the speed of stench spreading in a field of rain,
the speed of discovering a spud
that looks like a spud but isn't, hollowed
out with rot, like some sick joke played by the earth

And like some sick joke the cottiers
watched as their other crops of corn, and barley
and wheat and meat were loaded up onto the boats
and sailed to England and the less we say
of economics that were laissez-faire the better
and the less we use the term 'famine' the better

and the less we say of Charles Trevelyan
the better and the less we say of the soup kitchens
the dismal soup kitchens he introduced the better
and the less we say of the mother
at the head of the queue as the stirabout gruel runs out
the better and the less we say of the shipped-out mutton
and the pork and the poultry and the butter the better

Better to think of dawn's butter sky in Cove
or Cobh or Queenstown — call it what you will —
that unassuming harbour town in Cork
where ships set sail for Liverpool where ships
set sail for Canada, America, Australia, New Zealand
better to think of a mother and a daughter
who had walked their boots off to get there,
had made a journey to make a journey
out of here, out of hunger and into hope,
better to think of them walking up the gangplank,
embarking and chatting about the cottier husband
the father they'd left behind, the only photographs
of him were the photographs they'd gathered in their heads
the only written notes from him were written on the paper
of their hearts, their paper-thin hearts
as they set sail and watched St Colman's Cathedral on the hill
and Ireland erase themselves
in the descending morning mist

And in the descending morning mist
under the ship's skeletal rigging
shoulder to shoulder with the others onboard
who could blame them
for thinking they were through the worst of it
the days of waiting for one spud to come good,
to wake and wonder if today
would usher in a break in the weather

a week of uninterrupted sun
or at least a week of interrupted rain,
the look on her father's face, his temper,
tested, how she'd never heard him shout
like that, or known him so quiet around the house
as if it were infecting him, the fungus,
as on board, from Liverpool, Atlantic bound,
America bound, hot meal bound, full tummy bound,
bright lights bound, green grass bound,
future bound, life bound, survival bound,
the hell-away-from-Ireland bound
someone coughs and someone else
and nobody thinks anything of it

And nobody thinks of anything
until the second day and the realization
of the rations kick in, a pound of flour
and three quarts of water, water
stored in manky whiskey casks
and flour from drums ridden with god-knows-what
to be cooked on the fires above the deck
with everybody pushing in at once
to make their puny batch of stirabout
puny porridge of Indian cornmeal and rice
and soon the fevers set in and soon
the bodies and soon the bodies overboard
and soon the sharks surround the ship
and follow it, but soon America

And no sooner did America arrive
than America wanted them to leave
the mother and the daughter who
by some miracle had made it through
the typhus and the cholera
and the scraps and the stink and the sharks,

released from quarantine on Staten Island
to find themselves not welcome in Manhattan
wondering if they should have gone to Canada instead

Instead there was the Know-Nothing Party,
'No Irish Need Apply', the tenement slums,
a predominating Protestantism,
a fear of Catholics taking over, thoughts,
endless thoughts of home, the husband, father,
St Colman's Cathedral, as they swept
and cleaned the houses of the Upper East
together before returning to their room
at Five Points, the shanty town, Lower East
where one evening walking home
the mother bought a bottle of milk
from a street-stall vendor, so thirsty,
and with a little cash, the cold bottle's glass
in her hand, the liquid rushing through her throat
but what is that tang of chalk, ammonia, Swill?

It's Swill, that tang of chalk, ammonia,
was what the milkmen sold on the street
from stinking vats, the milk from dying cows
packaged with a fancy label, leaving
the mother to lie on her bed in their stinking digs,
kept alive for a little while longer
by visions, reminiscences of the potato fields
when they were full of white flowers, full
of her full husband hard at work, harvesting,
she harvested these memories, but left
to leave the world like that

To leave the world like that, to leave
her daughter to scatter her ashes
by the Lower Manhattan docks

the South Street Seaport looking back
in the direction from which they came
on the boats they've since called 'Coffin Ships'
as she remembers sailing by Long Island for a week,
its green fields recalling Cork, Youghal, her father,
before Lower Manhattan's skyline
honed into view, the spires of Trinity Church
ordained by King Billy in the 17th century
stood like the architectural equivalent
of 'Welcome to New York; Taigs Out'
as they held each other's hands
and made their way, hungry,
through the diseases of the city
to eke a living, hand to mouth

So, here's to the eked lives,
the hands and mouths
of the hand to mouth
who never made America, Australia,
the ones who knew the emptiness
of empty hands and mouths
the ones who never made it to the coast
of being sated, the other shore
across the water from their hunger

And across the water of hunger's history
we arrive in the present day,
the plentiful present day
where even a pandemic
cannot stop the great big gears
of agro-industry, the giant John Deere wheels
of the potato harvester ploughing on
in seemingly endless desert fields in China
responsible for a third of the world's output
with hundreds of thousands of metric tons

of French fries alone in '20/'21
unlike this patch of the Killyleagh Road
where now we arrive in the present day
a day of plenty enough
where the aforementioned grandfather
unearths a number of early British Queens
behind the pig shed
fills an old meal bucket full
and brings them to the kitchen
to his son, home with his wife
and sons for a summer holiday
from where they live in England,
he brings them to the kitchen
still with the soil on
and the son washes, then seasons,
then roasts them not turning them at all
not opening the oven once
so that the bottoms crisp up, almost burn —
a synonym for the Maillard reaction —
come off easily with a fish slice
and they sit at the table
with mayonnaise and tomato sauce
and they eat until the potatoes are history
and they themselves around a table
in a bungalow in County Down
with the grandfather 80 at the end of year
and still with his bowl of boiled spuds to himself
still steaming in the evening light
through the patio doors
are history too
this family who've taken their place
at the stretch or starve table of history,
the table of history where it must follow
that history is a history of the potato.

Supposed

You were supposed to come but didn't,
twenty-four weeks of Mum's womb-quiet your lot,
and I wonder about you now, sometimes:
was it you who kept the blades off the ride-on mower
when David accidentally ran me over,
were our string of runaway dogs running to you
down the Scaddy Road into eternity,
would you fidget next to me at church,
Sunday dinner, pass on pudding like Lynne,
eat meat first and leave your veg like Ruth,
empty, like Richard, the gravy boat,
like Dad, prize peace and quiet, the greenhouse,
or stay up like Mum to crochet for newborns?

The Tall Trees of the Killyleagh Road

They are the skeletons of my childhood
Like skeletons they watch over my childhood
On the hill, a line of trees, childhood's sentinels
I see them, their black bones on the horizon
They speak of another time, another Ireland
All my childhood, on the hill, the old trees queue
Who planted these trees which overlooked my infancy
What would they say, those black bones on winter sky
Speak, bones of earth, old bones of Ulster
Bones of childhood, bones of the horizon
They are not sentinels, these trees of my childhood
They are not trees of my childhood, these bare bones
So much of my life, these bony witnesses
Keeping watch, were they ash or sycamore
I'd never paid them much attention until now
They are not the trees of earth, these trees
Not of Ulster, nor of earth, these trees
No loveliness in these trees, nor cherries
Writing about trees again, the tall trees
I cannot rub these tall trees from my sight
Peopling the horizon of my mind, the tall trees
They were what fenced us in, these wooden witches
If they could speak, those sappy surveyors
In the way that most of the trees happen
What trees, what wind, what rain lapping their branches
O my trees, my tall trees, my sons and daughters
In the beginning there was the Killyleagh Road
For there is a spirit in the tall trees
Overcast, raining, I recall that hill of trees
They are not cutting down the great tall trees
A country's character is in its trees, these
A hundred thousand unlit fires, my childhood's trees
Playing late, we took them for granted, the trees
That barren, twisted hilltop, with the weird trees
They're singing in the wind, the tall trees, afterlife

The dead are singing in the tall trees, through their bones
Their black bones sing a song for the dead in the wind
They, the tall trees, are singing my song
I'm writing too much about the tall trees
Let me begin again with the tall trees, let me

To Angel, Islington

i.m. Roddy Lumsden

You summoned me termly, a Monday night,
to a plump poetry-loving Scot,
up massive moving stairs, through
the rush-hour traffic of the Tube
from Hainault, the dead end of the East End
of the Central Line, to come alive year-round,
proferring my latest dabblings in verse
to a band of pub-going night-classers.

Angel, where are you now, this Monday night,
a life away? Where is your enigmatic Celt?
Won't he bundle in, hair side-swept,
now as he did then, wearing the mac, late,
to a classroom full of windows full of London
night, Angel, London light, Angel, the done undone?

Failure

Confronted by myself in the back door's black glass,
perched on the island, morning, half-six,
I wonder: is bungee jumping vertigo's cure,
handling a spider arachnophobia's answer,
the market square the agoraphobe's antidote,
the car boot the claustrophobic's moment
of clarity? And then we come to failure,
whether more makes you a better loser?
How many losings does it take before
we get the hang of it, shake the fear?
How many mornings in the mirror
before we come to terms, recognize
that its face is our face, the face we wear
with a shirt and tie, like clockwork, clockwise.

'We returned to our places, these Kingdoms . . .'

. . . to find the townsfolk stuffing their faces
with pigs in blankets, Brussels sprouts, sauces,
one of red, foreign berries, one from bread —
creamy, nutmeggy, not a little divisive —
wearing paper crowns, glued to a king
on a mounted flat screen, delivering
his speechwriter's speech from autocue:
how horrible it must be for everyone,
given the high prices and issues,
he imagines, like feeding a family, offering
his thoughts. Millions hang on his words,
with brandy on their breaths, breaking wind
on sofas in centrally heated rooms —
scents of liqueur and brassica suffuse.

There are presents, wild-eyed, pyjama-ed children
and wrapping paper — we had never seen
so much wrapping. Fake smiles, discarded gifts,
terraces festooned with illuminations,
as arguments break out over word games
in dwellings full of hot, unpeopled rooms,
wi-fi connected voice-controlled devices,
leftovers, and boiling water taps, a people
clutching green bags full of numbered letters,
scoring points against each other.
There are times we long for that manger.

Tenants

I pull up a chair next to my bachelor self,
a little sojourn into the past, Bristol,
the big bay window in the rented flat.
We take note of the building's other residents
returning home: they claim their post,
you can hear them clomping up the stairs,
talking loudly on the phone to loved ones,
making dinner, the clang of pan on stove,
post-work debriefs with flatmates, arguments,
laughter, a bottle uncorked, sighs, slammed doors,
TV and an intermingling of children.
Tenants: have we ever been anything else
but over-paying, get-out clause inhabitants,
here for a bit, before the next place?

Portrait of Our Son Running Amok at Blenheim Palace

for Aimee

Running through the formal gardens, shouting,
skirting the edge of the fountain, rattling
Winston Churchill's front door needing the loo,
wanting wheelies in the pram, wanting down
when we're about to start our lunch, leaning
out of the carriage on the mini-railway
repeatedly, despite repeated warnings,
rushing everywhere, up the steps, to the gate,
through the hedge maze, to the bench, the bridge,
the car, everywhere, all of the time
correcting us with insouciance, bursting
into song randomly in public, refusing
to wear a coat, kicking off a sock, a shoe.
He resembles me at times; at times, you.

Jock the Silverback's View from Gorilla Island, Bristol Zoo

Here we go again, the 12.30 lot;
Gorillas: Live Feeding and Talk —
Watch Jock the Silverback in Action.
Here they come, flocking six deep, jostling —
the shorter ones on tippy toes —
for a good gawp, zooming-in devices
across the separating pond, capturing
my ennui in HD.
Sharp intakes of breath when I beat my chest
or scale a pole or throw a log
or something other than stay stock-still.
I scratch my head, my ear, my back, my ass,
and still they snap and gawk, conferring.

Who do they think they are?

Their inked limbs, I see them, guzzling
drinks from lidded cardboard cups, in flimsy,
unseasonable clothing, garish, loud,
always wanting a spot up front, blank-faced,
chomping processed food from boxes,
threatening, in short, but strangely passive —
the young on the shoulders of the old
demanding ice cream and the swings.

Lunch is an iceberg lettuce, lobbed
whole by the part-timers in green polos
as the Tannoy trots out the same old facts: *vegetarians . . .*
hand reared . . . blah blah blah.
Most leave before the end,
some stay, head tilted, gormless, stare,
as if I seem somehow familiar.

To Lime Pickle

Epitome of pizzazz, apotheosis
of citrus,

firecracker
poppadom ambassador,

you are
a tightrope walk between here and a star

of funky heat,
your flesh a punchy, hit-me beat

in a hit song
about what someone did all summer long

in a hot country
in their youth; you are a walk-in pantry,

lip-smacker starter, beer washed down bounty;
if flavour was a state, or county.

Killyleagh Road Pastoral

The only intrusion
was Sunday evening summer light
over the Robinsons' field,
ricocheting off my father
and his greenhouse,
locking up his seedlings
for the night.

The only smoke
was bonfire,
cuttings of the whin
by the pig shed
no longer used for pigs
near the strawberries.

The only flash
was the sun setting
behind the massive ash
a field away
as it caught a face
in a window
of a pebble-dashed bungalow.

The only bang
the backfiring
of the lawnmower.

The only gunshot
the farmer's
at the myxomatosis
rabbit.

The only cinders
last night's coal

in the grate, cold,
in the living room.

The only loss, time,
the only marching time,
that time.

'THE TIME IS SHORT'

i.m. Tom Parker

His solitary Sunday-cigarette smoke
about the patio

would linger
long after

five
when they'd make the drive

away home — my aunty
and he —

to Comber through Ballygowan
past the church — Presbyterian —

with four white words, proud
above its clock, in capitals, loud

like this note of tobacco
that won't mellow.

In Praise of Blank Verse

The thing I love about blank verse is everything
that's loved can be set down so lovingly,
so freely, such as bread and jam and butter
in this iambic gamesmanship of meter,
the pleasure of playing within the rules,
against the laws, taking stresses to the limits
of the line and back again. There needn't be
an angle, or agenda; let the zeitgeist
go to hell, may tokenism take a running
jump, for now the truth is in the *thud*
thud, thud of the universal's heartbeat
just as it was ages ago, for Milton,
Wordsworth, Coleridge, for whom it came so
easily, like 'Frost at Midnight', for example,
or boat stealing from 'Book I' of *The Prelude*,
the serpent's speech in *Paradise Lost*
in which the fall of man is captured
in this relentless *dum-di-dum-di-dum*.
I've often thought it's freer than free verse,
resembling, though, a seismograph of the mind,
the fits and starts of the imagination
between the padded walls of pentameter.

I love it in the way I love the hills
of Killyleagh in autumn, each leaf-strewn
bend of road around the Quoile, my son
at the end of this October morning's garden
cycling through the names of all the colours,
an egg yolk bursting over toast, the randomness
of memory, the way it wants to make
each beat as natural as wildflowers
that punctuate late summer's uncut lawn.

And I love the way it lets me love you, love,
from the lamp-lit corner of this quiet room,

our wall of photographs in front of me:
the Giant's Causeway, Cave Hill, Bristol,
a sonogram of our second child. This life.

Lessons of the Master

i.m. Ciaran Carson

He told me straight
regarding my first manuscript

in Belfast, Bookfinders café,
over strong, filtered coffee

and handed out this feedback:
draft, check a dictionary, polish your tan brogues black —

referred to how his own
were all the better for it, Crockett & Jones —

the process will embolden,
he said, the punched pattern,

tone down the original rawness.
Still the apprentice

I recall his advice, Yeats, stitches,
well-made shoes, I look up *magnanimous.*

At the Wallace Collection

Take Frans Hals and Rembrandt,
to think of such Old Masters fussing
over these selfsame canvases, brushing,
withdrawing, sizing up, furrowing brows,
wondering whether to risk another stroke,
talking, drinking coffee near them, breathing,

the sound of horse and cart on cobblestone
in the street beneath, the comings and goings
of people trying to make ends meet,
the shouts and smells of market day maybe,
conversations of workplace tensions,
a lousy government, confessions

of parental guilt, talk of rising prices,
political unrest, investment tips —
I'm telling you, it's all about tulips —
drifting up to meet these draughtsmen, candlelit
in their patronized, ramshackle, dim studios,
giving up, for now, and going for an early lunch

through streets which aren't just streets to them
but phenomena of light and shade, hundreds
of hues, to a café where a bowl of fruit,
translucence, tint of wine, the golden,
black and white crust of the bread, canals,
the rippling water afternoon is all too much,

the world so vivid they can barely watch.

Dear John

i.m. John Lavery

I'm writing this while listening to 'The Swan' —
Saint-Saëns, did Hazel ever introduce you? —
and looking at your Sutton Courtenay paintings:
'The Wharf', 'A Writing Room', 'Summer on the River',
'The Hall of the Manor House' . . . To think
we rented Penny Cottage, next to where you stayed
with the Asquiths, 1917. I wanted to write
to say you got it perfectly, the light,
the luxurious overhang
of the branches on the languorous water,
jetties from back gardens, the privilege
of the swans, distant yet watchful, their white,
how the punts nudge each other, the pole
at rest in the shingly riverbed. I think
of the lady in the boat, the one reclining
reading or writing or drawing, the man
in the boater and full cream linen suit, the dog,
and all of this while war raged on elsewhere
like Passchendaele. It's a pitch-perfect portrait
of the oblivious, the ignorant.

It hasn't changed, the river path, I thought
you'd like to know. More boats, of course,
engine-powered, fewer punts, but the swans
still swim, congregate, hiss, protect their young.
I thought you'd like to know I bring my son
to pick the plums in autumn; you'd like
their shades of red and yellow. I've written one
about him here, becoming a father.
As I write this, I'm remembering Kathleen,
your late first wife, and Eileen, your daughter.

There is still peace to be found in this world,
peace as peaceful as your Sutton Courtenay river,
a sense of something to be sought after
despite the odds, worked for
as in your 'Writing Room', the hunched figure, alone,
pen on paper in the dying light of evening by a window.
Dear John, I thought you'd like to know.

The Stream at Steventon

for Rory

Remember the stream at Steventon, our go-to
afternoon by The Green, where I took you
on the back of the racer down that rat run
of a road, through the echoing underpass, noisy,
past the tip, and out-of-business bakery
where you'd snaffled the currant hedgehog bun?
I'd lean the bike against an ivied tree,
summer holiday, nobody but you and me:

our feeble dams, the twigs we'd race, segments
of orange, Braeburn mouthful chats, impressions
of presenters as we spotted slug or crayfish,
our thrown stones, dens, the key we found together,
imagined it unlocking a door to somewhere,
a stream, perhaps, we'd cycle to, play at forever.

The Listening Swan

They claim, in Finnish folklore,
      it's a divine ancestor, messenger
between the here and hereafter

and when it dips its arrow-like head under
      it's communicating with this world's other,
back and forth, as river's sole interpreter,

translator, fluent in the dead language of water,
      its incessant muttering, a yammer —
try as we might — we cannot quite decipher.

Death of an Artisan

from *The Lost Poems of Georges Bertrand*

i.m. Guillaume

THE BAKERY GIG

It was my teenage summer job, the last resort.
I left it late and all my friends had nabbed
the waiting jobs, the bar jobs, in short
the jobs with tips and regular hours.
Nobody wanted the bakery gig.
Ridiculously early starts, long shifts,
in a basement, leaving you too knackered
to go out drinking in the evening.
I had decided to hate it
before I even got the job.
My mother saw the advert in a window
walking home through town
getting her groceries one Saturday morning.
Georges, it'll have to do. I will not tolerate
you sitting on your ass all summer long.
And so, I went along for an interview.

GUILLAUME

He was new in the area,
Guillaume, a pastry chef,
the youngest to achieve
the 'Meilleur Ouvrier de France',
but wanted out of Paris
to branch out on his own,
a bigger place for his wife and kids,
fresh air, a house with a garden,
drawn to the heritage of Lyon —

Marie Bourgeois, La Mère Brazier,
Paul Bocuse, the *bouchons* —
wanted to break away from his boss,
a celebrity Michelin-starred chef
more interested in media appearances,
establishing cheapening franchises,
than the daily grind at the pass.

And so he found himself
in our sleepy, satellite, market town,
living with his family above his bakery,
the bakery he spent the first year renovating,
the old bakery he made the new bakery,
the bakery which, back in the day,
used to be an age-old family-run patisserie
but hadn't seen as much as a tartlet in years
not since the last incumbent packed it in,
couldn't stand the competition
from Rousseau's, the chain
which sold big tasteless loaves —
pain ordinaire —
of bleached white flour with additives
cheaply, and pastry made with margarine and oils
and cakes that tasted chiefly of sugar,
vats mixed by machines in a warehouse
out of town and distributed for retail
in polythene, at a peppercorn price
throughout the province;
but the locals lapped it up,
wouldn't hear a bad word said about the place,
and who could blame them
with low wages and mouths to feed?
The odds were stacked against him from the start.
Insisting on only flour and salt and water and yeast,
timelessness over trendiness

and everything made on his own premises
he was *Le Décret Pain* of 1993
before it was decreed.

I remember entering, the afternoon,
arriving at the shopfront,
ducking under the half-closed shutters
to let myself in, no sign of anyone.
I called out, *Monsieur? Hello?*
I'm here for the interview.
Down here, came his voice, returning
from the basement kitchen,
you're late before you've even begun.

FIRST IMPRESSIONS

White is the colour I recall
when I think of it, that kitchen. The walls,
the brick bond tiles, the drums of flours, sugars,
the fluorescent tube lights, aprons, even the tea towels,
and, of course, Guillaume,
too modern for a cravat or toque blanche,
not quite 'Le Chef de l'Hôtel Chatham, Paris'
in that portrait by William Orpen,
yet in his classic double-breasted chef's jacket,
the view of the back of his white-haired head,
hulking figure hunched over a counter,
his pallor, his face the shade of wan
unique to the night-shift strip-lit subterranean,
not looking up,
continuing mixing or kneading a white dough,
he called me into his night white underworld
out of my white bright day.

IMPRINT

You must be Georges, he said, looking up
momentarily as his scraper hovered
over a bulk of dough about to be divided. *Well Georges*,
he said, *let's start at the beginning:*
The first rule of the bakery is
don't wear black. And with his hand
just dipped in a bin of flour
he slapped me on the back.

MISE EN PLACE

Before you learn to make a baguette, he said,
you have to learn to make a loaf, but
before you learn to make a loaf . . .
what? he asked.
I shrugged. *Before we learn to knead,*
or mix a cake, or contemplate a solitary petit four,
you need to learn to clean, respect
the space you work in, respect the others
in the kitchen, respect the produce, respect
the dough, the bread, the customer. Everything
flows from a clean and tidy worktop.
There is no creativity without, at first, order,
clearing the decks. We clean and arrange our minds
when we sweep and mop the floor. Get to it.
Before long you will see beauty
in a room of spotless stainless steel.

He handed me the brush and I hated him
in the way the ignorant hate those
who only mean them well, who only mean
to teach them, lead them out of their unknowing.

But to me, I'd come to work in a bakery,
and all I would be doing
was sweeping the flour
from the floor.

MOTHER DOUGH

Huge, she resided in a lidded plastic cuboidal container
on wheels in the coldest,
darkest corner of the kitchen, and yet
Guillaume loved her with all his heart,
checked up on her almost every hour —
he'd peak inside, nod to himself and carry on.

Every day it was my job to feed her,
discard yesterday's growth,
then add equal quantities of flour and water,
give a thorough stir with the 4-foot paddle
to keep her bubbling, alive. *Georges,* he quipped,
whatever you do, don't kill my mother!
Without her we are screwed. And plus,
he added, *I've practically kept her all my life.*

Flour, water, and the air's bacteria in a tub:
beautiful cesspit, sour soul of yeast, years
of attention, addition, adoration,
nail-polish-remover scented sludge
mixed in a massive bucket, miraculous
concoction of barely anything, life-giver
always on the verge of dying, swampy quicksand
keeping the bakery afloat, bubbly beginner
of tang, crust, crumb, flavour, rise — mother.

HOW TO BAKE A LOAF

Stacking the proofing baskets
to dry on top of the deck ovens
I used to watch him, the speed of his hands,
his head bowed, the dough-scraper clacking away,
the gentle
slap of the slab of dough
as he coaxed it out of the proofing container,
cut, portioned, weighed,
manoeuvred each ball
for its second rise, air pockets trying
to break through the tension
of each incipient crust. He didn't believe
in knocking back the dough too much.
You'll see some who take their fist and smash
the bulk like a punchbag, he'd say.
They've got it wrong. You mustn't.
Gently, gently, gently, he'd instruct.
What has it done to you? Remember, he said,
the most important element of good bread,
he said, *is air and we incorporate it*
into everything we do.
Imagine, he said, *a loaf so light it floats*
out of the oven right onto your carving block . . .
Now, aim for that. Or think, he said, *of the swan*
in that piece, he said, *by Saint-Saëns.*

GUILLAUME'S KITCHEN

When most think of a professional kitchen
or bakery they think of a large ape at the pass,
gravel-voiced, grisly, stubbled, sweaty,
shouty, sweary, asserting himself

by reprimanding someone else's failure
publicly, telling an underling
to do a task again, a picture of disdain.
When most think of a professional kitchen
they think of fire, speed, noise, a kind
of hell, 'egotism', 'masculinity' might come to mind,

but when I think of Guillaume's kitchen
I think of a calmness akin to a garden
on a summer's night, a full moon
fully visible, fat on its flat pond, how
as the last batch baked he'd mop the floors
himself, I think of the steady purpose
with which fruit ripens on a tree in the dark,
a certain sunlight that makes you walk outside.

Lightness, richness, delicateness;
if mixed, proved and baked right, not a trace
of butter should remain on your fingers.
I think of him teaching me the ways of brioche;
how instead I learned something of manliness.

OVEN

Was there anything as black
as the inside of Guillaume's electric deck ovens
when the doors were closed and the heat was high
and the breads were baking, the orange pilot light
burning bright? What was their dark art
of light loaves, rise and fall, crusts browned and burst?
Don't open those, whatever you do,
he'd say, as if keeping it from me, as if he knew.

GUILLAUME'S PASTRY

His life's ambition
was to roll it out so thin
that through it, on each occasion,
you could read, sans interruption,
his local paper, *Le Progrès Lyon*.

TARTE TATIN

His favourites were surprisingly simple,
homely, such as Tarte Tatin. He favoured
Cox's Orange Pippins which kept their shape
and aromatic flavour when baked; they married well
with the caramel. *The richness*, he'd say,
see the lamination of the pastry,
the evaporation of the butter between layers,
see the colour of the apples in the caramel,
a deep gold. Unearthly gold,
the colour of gold before gold becomes
the colour of burnt, the taste of apple
before it tastes no longer of apple.
See? Guillaume, I can see them now.

SUGAR WORK

It was a lesson in concentration,
focus. Nothing was as bitter as sugar
left too long to caramelize, or cooked
too high, too fast. *You've got to keep your eye on it.*
In a second it could go from golden brown
to black, bubble up like hot tar
and be damned.

There's nothing like sugar work, he'd say,
to teach you a thing or two about time
and, showing both his hands, *how it scalds*.

'AND WHAT TIME DO YOU CALL THIS?'

I could talk of the silence, the sky, birdsong
as I whizzed through the empty streets
on my father's old racer, the chill of the air
as I leant above the bullhorn handlebar,
not even a sign of the street sweeper,
the field of flax flowers long closed over,
but 3 a.m. is the hour of what exactly?

It seemed that time itself was asleep those mornings
as I set out in good time for my shift
belted through the town over
the cobbled square, down the alley
to the bakery's back door, dismounted,
my heart racing in the dead of night,
of morning, the dead of in-between time,
the dead of the deadest, ungodliest of hours
or whatever the hell you want to call that time,
that time where hands met flour met water
met salt met yeast met time met Guillaume
who'd meet me, every time, with the same old line.

QUIGNON

Twisting off the *quignon*,
the tip, one of the pointy ends
of a baguette
I'd left to the side

marked the end of my shift,
a day's weighing and kneading
and cleaning and sweeping.
And nothing tasted like it
every time
I walked outside
to the fresh air, fresh light,
to the fresh, light, on air feeling
of finishing work,
nearing the end of adolescence,
to tear through another afternoon
of my life's *quignon.*

ON SIMPLICITY

Just water, flour, salt, yeast and time,
he'd say, shaking his head,
feet up on the bistro table out the back,
eating his afterwork baguette,
considering a slice
like Hamlet
with Yorick's skull,
as he added,
its open crumb
catching the light,
a web, labyrinthine,
alveolate,
and yet, Georges,
and yet . . .

THE WAY OF BREAD

I'd love to say he found it easy,
how the townsfolk flocked to him in droves,
queued out the door, around the corner
back to the marketplace
for his croissant, *baguette de tradition*,
how he employed more staff to cope
with surges in demand, how he had to rent
a bigger premises, achieved acclaim
in the community instantaneously
but no, it wasn't like that at all.

If faith were ever a measurement of time
it was the time it took Guillaume
to turn the town to his way of thinking
which was the way of the hand, the way
of the imagination, the way of a toddler
on a Saturday morning walking out of the shop
with chocolate all over their face, the way
of the early riser and late-nighter, often
it was the empty-handed way, the hard way,
the heart's and soul's way, a very human way,
a simple way, the way of bread's way.

A FIRE

I was near the end of my first year
at university in Paris when I got the call.
My mother phoned as soon as she heard.
A fire, she said, *the bakery*, she said, *Guillaume*,
she said. *It wasn't entirely clear*, she said.
At least the children made it out, she said.

What happens to the gifts of the gifted
when the gifted go? How Guillaume moved his hands,
flicked flour across the counter,
his swift, angled incisions through the dough
with his grignette to get an enormous ear
on the crust of a *pain de campagne*
like that, like nobody else in France.
Remember to call when you get back from Paris
were his last words to me,
and what did I tell you about wearing black?
as one last time his floury hand thwacked my back.

THE SINGING BREAD

This morning, nearing my fiftieth year
before I went for a check-up
on that shadow blooming in my lungs,
I left a dough to rise
in the round lined wicker banneton —
one of his grandfather's —
he'd given me before my move to Paris,
a simple white dough, which I shaped
and proved again when I returned,
then baked, the oven on full, steamed up,
boule on the cast-iron stone, waiting
for the gold and the black and the yellow
of the crust he used to preach about, promised —
patience, he'd repeat, *is the difference* —
the enormous ear only possible
in a powerful professional oven —
then left it to cool,
listening to its crust contract, *le pain qui chante*,
the singing bread, as it breathed its heat
on my cheek, then left it to cool again,

then ate with butter, then washed, dried,
tidied away my implements,
swept and mopped the floor,
wiped the countertops
wondering again if I had met his standards,
if he'd be pleased with this effort,
before I sat, sat to sweep and mop
and arrange these memories
of this baker's life baked into mine,
these words left like semolina on the tray
when the loaf's ready, been lifted away.

Notes and Acknowledgements

A recording of 'The Swan' (*The Carnival of the Animals*, R 125: XIII, Camille Saint-Saëns), arranged for cello and piano, by Yo-Yo Ma and Kathryn Stott (*Songs from the Arc of Life*, Sony Music Classical, 2015) features in 'Listening to "The Swan"' and other poems throughout the book.

page 38 The following helped to inform this poem:
Gallagher, M and P and Mac Con Iomaire, Máirtín, 'The History of the Potato in Irish Cuisine and Culture' in Friedland, S (ed) *Vegetables: Proceedings of the Oxford Symposium on Food and Cookery 2008*, Devon, Prospect Books.
McNeill, William H, 'The Introduction of the Potato into Ireland', *The Journal of Modern History*, 21, no. 3 (1949): 218–22
O'Connell, Helen, 'Bleak Food: William Wilde, Famine and Gastronomy', *Canadian Journal of Irish Studies*, 41(2018): 156-178
https://www.irishtimes.com/culture/scary-tales-of-new-york-life-in-the-irish-slums-1.1335816
https://www.crf-usa.org/bill-of-rights-in-action/bria-26-2-the-potato-famine-and-irish-immigration-to-america.html
page 56 The title is a line from T S Eliot's 'The Journey of the Magi'.
page 72 A translation of Georges Bertrand's last poem 'Le Morte d'Artisan'.

Thanks are due to the editors of *Poetry London* and *Reading Poets: An Anthology* (Two Rivers Press) where some of these poems or versions of them were published first. 'Teaching English' was placed in the Kent and Sussex Open Poetry Competition 2023; thanks to the judge, Jonathan Edwards. 'Lessons of the Master' was selected as part of 'Last Night's Fun', The Poetry Jukebox's Ciaran Carson curation, featuring in Belfast and Paris.

I thank David Briggs, Niall Campbell, Peter Robinson and Ben Wilkinson for their editorial advice and encouragement.

I'm grateful to Peter Fallon and to his colleagues at The Gallery Press for all they've done to bring this book to publication.